Gather

LIKE A

goddess

AN ILLUSTRATED GUIDE TO STARTING
a women's circle

GATHER LIKE A GODDESS

An Illustrated Guide to Starting A Women's Circle

Written & Illustrated by Holli Rae

HOLLIRAE.COM

Featuring artwork from The Goddess Project film, created by: Charlotte Apers, Lia Gonzalez, Min Liu, Jeca Martinez & Heather Kai Smith.

THEGODDESSPROJECT.COM

facebook.com/thegoddessproject

instagram.com/thegoddessproject

. . . .

. . . .

Post Pictures of Your Circle
WITH #LIKEAGODDESS
so we can find you and show you some *love!*

HELLO BEAUTIFUL,

I hope this guide is helpful for you!

Over the last decade, I've met so many incredible women empowering themselves and their communities through the practice of reoccurring women's circles.

Sisterhood is potent and storytelling can change the world. I've had and witnessed countless epiphanies and incredible transformations through women gathering together in safe spaces.

We created The Goddess Project documentary to amplify the voices of women. After over 200 screenings of the film globally, it has also proven to be a powerful tool to bring people together, start conversations and create lasting connections. People like you are using the movie to inspire people and to develop curriculum, event programming, live experiences and more.

That is why I decided to illustrate this information and outline some ideas for you to consider! Women have been gathering in circles for centuries but we can take our connections to the next level with the modern tools we have access to today.

Each circle is unique, and that is what is so fun - you can make it your own! This guide is full of my favorite experiences I've had so far at gatherings around the world. Take what resonates with you, leave what doesn't, add your own spice and have fun!

With all my love,

Holli

MAGIC

happens when

WOMEN

gather

WHAT IS A WOMEN'S CIRCLE?

With the chaos of navigating our world, a women's circle is a safe space for women to come together, share their voices and to be heard and seen.

Since the beginning of time, women have gathered in circles to empower each other, exchange wisdom and co-create together.

These uplifting gatherings help women build community, embrace their feminine power and set intentions for the kind of world they would like to see and create.

This illustrated how-to guide will help you facilitate memorable, transformative experiences for women and girls in your community!

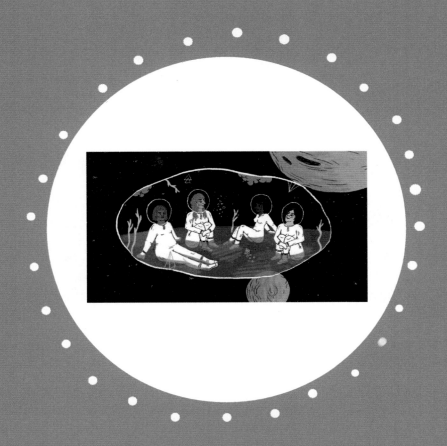

FORMING A CIRCLE

Invite your friends or put a call out to meet new women! Social media, community spaces and meet-up groups are great places to get the word out about your circle. Posters and flyers can also go a long way when posted in local shops and businesses.

If you have a mailing list or a collaborator who does, send out an email invitation. You can also create a website or Facebook event page and ask women to invite their friends. There are infinite ways to spread the word, including good old fashioned word-of-mouth!

You'll be surprised how many women will show up looking for sisterhood in your city!

 find

YOUR COMMUNITY!

If this is your first gathering, consider hosting a screening of **The Goddess Project** as an icebreaker. Invite people to come together for an inspiring movie night at your home, local cinema or community space.

This film gets people talking, so having a Q&A afterwards is a great way to gather feedback about planning future events! You can put up a big poster board to write on, or take notes with each person's thoughts.

HERE ARE SOME QUESTIONS YOU CAN ASK TO BRAINSTORM IDEAS:

How often shall we meet?

Who will organize and where?

What topics would you like to discuss?

What types of activities shall we do?

Would you like to help host?

REMEMBER TO COLLECT EVERYONE'S CONTACT INFORMATION SO YOU CAN STAY IN TOUCH!

USING THE FILM AS A TOOL TO HELP GUIDE YOUR CIRCLES

The Goddess Project documentary is 101 minutes long and was created for teens and adults.

Some of the topics covered in the film are self-discovery, travel, menstruation, sisterhood, the media & its influence, healing from trauma & abuse, creativity, sustainability and pursuing your dreams.

If you feel inspired by the messages of the film, you can use it to help guide activities and discussions in your circles!

goddess

....

....

....

....

....

....

....

....

....

....

....

....

....

Guest List

....
....
....
....
....
....
....
....
....
....
....
....
....

how to ORGANIZE

Circles usually occur once a month and last between 2-5 hours. A group of 4 to 50 women is recommended and the smaller the group is, the more time everyone will have to get to know each other.

Focusing each circle on a unique theme is a great way to stay on track and guide each event. Keep reading for themes and discussion questions you can use to facilitate different circle experiences!

THEMES FROM THE FILM

TAKING THE LEAP
Have you taken a leap of faith to follow your intuition?

THE JOURNEY OF SELF-DISCOVERY
What have you learned about yourself along your life journey?

THE POWER OF INFLUENCE
Who or what influences you?
How do you influence others?

SISTERHOOD
Why is sisterhood important?
How can we support each other?

TRAUMA & HEALING
Have you experienced pain, trauma or abuse?
What can we do to heal?

WE'RE ALL ONE
How can we create more unity and love in the world around us?

THE DIVINE FEMININE
How do you celebrate and embody the feminine?

CREATION
We birth projects, ideas, businesses, babies & more.
What are you most passionate about creating in life?

LIVING YOUR TRUTH
What is your calling?
When do you feel most true to yourself?

CIRCLE THEMES

GOALS
What intention are you ready to set? Write down where you want to be in 1 month, 1 year and 5 years.

WOMANHOOD
What has been your experience being a woman?

NATURE
What is your relationship to nature?
When do you feel the most wild and free?

GRATITUDE
What are you grateful for?
How can we practice gratitude more often?

FEMINISM & POWER
How do you define feminism & women's empowerment?

CREATIVITY
What mediums do you use to express yourself?
How does creating make you feel?

YOUNGER SELF
What advice would you give to your younger self?

GROWING UP
How has your childhood shaped who you are? How are you growing or wanting to grow at this stage of your life?

MENSTRUATION
What has been your experience with bleeding and your period?

ELDERS
What are your mother's and grandmother's traits?
How are they reflected in you?

& DISCUSSION TOPICS

REFLECTION
When do you feel most beautiful? Do others see you differently than you see yourself?

NOURISHMENT
What is your relationship with self care and food?
How do you spend your time and what do you consume?

MANIFESTATION
What do you want to attract and create?

RELATIONSHIPS
How do your relationships impact your daily life?

DREAMS
What are your dreams like?
How often do you remember and reflect on them?

ABUNDANCE
Are you living an abundant life?
How does this impact your sense of optimism?

LOVE
Do you feel loved? Who has helped you to know and experience true love?

DEATH & ENDINGS
How do you deal with the death of people, relationships & situations? How does the subject of death make you feel?

REBIRTH
How can we evolve after pain or loss?
Have you ever reinvented yourself?

VISION
What kind of vision do you have for yourself & our planet?

theme ideas

....

....

....

....

....

....

....

....

....

....

....

....

....

discussion topics

....

....

....

....

....

....

....

....

....

....

....

....

day of CIRCLE

Make sure you are well rested for this transformative day! If you are hosting or guiding the circle, you can take notes on what you would like to say and how you would like the event to flow. It is also helpful to outline a schedule of how much time you will allot for activities and discussions.

schedule

TIMING YOUR CIRCLE

Below is an outline for how you can divide your time, based on what activities and themes you choose. Feel free to adjust it with your needs!

+ ARRIVAL WINDOW TO FIND SEATS
15-30 minutes

+ INTRODUCTION
30 minutes

+ JOURNALING + MEDITATION
15-20 minutes

+ DANCE + MOVEMENT
5-30 minutes

+ DISCUSSION + ACTIVITIES
1-3 hours

+ CLOSING + CLEANING UP THE CIRCLE
30 minutes

SETTING UP THE SPACE

Gather the supplies you'll need for your event and set
them up ahead of time. Arrange pillows or bolsters
in a circle, or ask your guests to bring a yoga mat
or cushion to sit on. You can use chairs as well if
you prefer not to sit on the floor. Blankets and comfy
clothes are always advised. Set up the environment in
whatever way works best for your space, but a circle
is recommended as the ideal seating arrangement
so everyone feels equal and can face each other.
Create a centerpiece in the middle with special
objects, flowers candles or lights. You can also make
it a community effort by having guests bring flowers
or special items to contribute to the space. Make a
music playlist ahead of time with a mix of uplifting and
relaxing tunes to help set the vibe of your circle.

checklist ☑

- [ ] ....
- [ ] ....
- [ ] ....
- [ ] ....
- [ ] ....
- [ ] ....
- [ ] ....
- [ ] ....
- [ ] ....
- [ ] ....
- [ ] ....
- [ ] ....
- [ ] ....
- [ ] ....

hello!

MY NAME IS...

INTRODUCE YOURSELVES AND SET AN INTENTION

When everyone has arrived, introduce yourself and share why you feel called to host the circle. Let the group know the structure and theme of the circle. For example: "This circle is a private space for all of us to be seen and heard without judgment. All sharing in here will be kept confidential between sisters. Each event will explore a different theme.
This week's theme is _____."

Make sure to include yourself in all of the sharing exercises so the space feels unified and safe.

Going clockwise around the room, have each woman share her name and intention for the circle.

CIRCLE *activities* & EXERCISES

MEDITATION

Share your own guided meditation or find one online that pairs well with your circle's theme. Ask all the women to close their eyes while breathing deeply in and out for the duration of the meditation.

JOURNALING

Try and start each circle by having the group journal about the theme. This makes time for everyone to become centered and contemplate what they will share. You can say, "Please take a moment for the next 3-5 minutes to journal about this subject and what it brings up for you."

PRACTICING LISTENING WITH A TALKING STICK

Sharing our individual stories makes us feel heard and less alone. By taking the time to be mindful and listen to what another woman has to share, we can show up for them in the most authentic way. A talking stick (or small a small object that can be passed around) is a great way to practice listening and to signify whose turn it is to talk in the circle. If a sister does not feel like sharing, she can always pass the talking stick. The person with the talking stick is the only one speaking at that time and it is everyone else's time to listen. Pass the object clockwise and let each person know how much time there will be to talk. For example, "I will start the circle by passing around the talking stick. Each woman has approximately ___ minutes to share."

MOVEMENT & MUSIC

There is nothing better than shaking it with your sisters. Put on a tune and get your groove on, or play music together. This is a great activity to do at the beginning and end of circles, as well as in between discussion topics when emotions are high and things can get heavy. Shake it off and belt it out for a couple of minutes!

BREATHWORK

Consider leading a group breathing exercise like the "Breath of Fire" or other focused breathing technique to get oxygen flowing at the beginning of your circle or in between discussions.

HIKING & NATURE

Start your circle with a hike in nature or consider hosting it in an outdoor setting like your backyard or at the beach with a fire pit. Being connected to the earth grounds us, and what better way to circle then being under the sun, moon and stars?!

POTLUCK

It is always great to connect over food. Consider starting or ending your circle with a meal or snacks and have everyone bring something to contribute. You can schedule a sit down meal or leave the food out and invite women to nourish themselves throughout the event.

YOGA & STRETCHING

Incorporate a yoga or stretching practice into your
circle. Consider leading this yourself or inviting a
teacher to help facilitate this. Beginning the circle with
a couple of simple stretches can help create a relaxed
mood. This gets everyone feeling into their bodies and
off to a positive start!

SEED PLANTING

Gather seeds from a local farmer, garden shop, or ask each woman to bring a pack of seeds. Bring soil and potting materials to the circle and invite everyone to set intentions and plant seeds together. It is said that if you put a seed under your tongue to water it for 8 minutes while envisioning your optimal heath and dreams, it will grow to nourish and support you once planted and tended to by you.

MIRROR WORK

Have each woman bring a small mirror for a self-reflective meditation. Find a mantra, poem or recording to guide the women towards looking within and developing self-love. Then have everyone share what they discovered in the mirror.

MAKING ARTS & CRAFTS

Making art together is a great way to play and express yourselves. Bring craft supplies and explore your creativity! Jewelry, Clay, Painting, Drawing and Collage are all fun group activities.

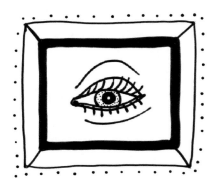

VISION BOARDS

A vision board is a manifestation tool to help bring your dreams to life. Create a board that you can look at everyday out of collaged images on a poster or in a frame. Ask all of the women to bring magazines that can be cut up, scissors and paintbrushes. Pick up some Mod-podge and start envisioning!

EYE CONTACT

Have women partner up and look into each others eyes in silence for 2-5 minutes. Then have each person share what they see in one another.

CARD DECKS

Bring a deck of Goddess, Gratitude or Tarot cards and spread them around the centerpiece of the circle. Invite all of the women to pick a card at the beginning of the circle before Journaling. After discussing what the card brings up for them, you can have them keep it or return it to your deck.

BATH SALT OFFERING

Gather a large bag of Epson Salts, a big bowl and spoons. Ask each woman to bring something to contribute to a Soak Mix like flower petals, herbs & essential oils. Place the bowl in the center of the circle and invite the women to mix in their offerings as they find their seats at the beginning of the event. At the end of the circle, pass out jars or ask them to bring their own to fill with the community Salt Offering to take home. Soak in the magic of the circle for days!

SISTER STRING

Find a large spool of yarn or string big enough to go around the room. At the end of your Sister Circle, pass the spool around clockwise and have each woman wrap it around her wrist. Once the circle is formed, cut the string at your wrist and pass scissors around to have every other woman do this as well. Have each woman tie her string around her wrist to keep as a symbol of the group's connectedness.

SPECIAL GUEST

Invite a musician, artist, expert, community leader or performer to attend your event and lead a discussion or teach a class. The possibilities are endless!

IDEAS

....

....

....

....

....

....

....

....

....

....

....

....

....

CLOSING
the CIRCLE

You can close the event with a reflection on the experience, a meditation, activity, dance or potluck. Mix it up every time!

Make sure to take a moment to thank everyone involved for showing up and contributing to the circle. Until next time, sisters!

Notes

....

....

....

....

....

....

....

....

....

....

....

....

....

Doodles

. . . ♡ . . .

· · · ♡ · · ·

. . . ♡ . . . .

· · · ♡ · · ·

· · · ♡ · · ·

LEARN MORE ABOUT
THE goddess PROJECT
AND STAY UP TO DATE!

WEBSITE
thegoddessproject.com

FACEBOOK
facebook.com/thegoddessproject

INSTAGRAM
instagram.com/thegoddessproject

LEARN MORE ABOUT

Holli Rae

AND STAY UP TO DATE!

WEBSITE
hollirae.com

INSTAGRAM
instagram.com/holli.rae